MY WORDS ARE SPIRIT AND LIFE

"Meditation is a special way of praying. . . . There are various methods of praying. Vocal prayer uses the spoken word; meditation, in general, uses less of the spoken word, but means to think about, to dwell on some phase of the Divine truth, on Christ, on some event in his life, and on the mysteries of salvation. In meditating we are to use all our powers of mind, soul, understanding, testing, imagination: to get images of hope, feelings, will and heart."

Thus does Stephanie M. Herz explain her understanding of meditation. She then goes on to map out a way of meditating that can be very attractive to today's Christians as we rediscover the Scriptures as a source of inspiration. Her meditations are based on the biblical passages that are used in the Liturgy of the Word for the Masses for Sundays and feast days of the Church year, as proclaimed by Vatican Council II. Surrounding each of these passages, which are called meditation clauses, Dr. Herz has selected a prayer addressed to Jesus Christ, thereby concentrating our meditation on Christ, making him the center of our life, our thinking, our feeling, and our actions.

For each Sunday or feast day, there are three groups of five meditation clauses, one group to correspond to each year in the liturgical cycle. Each meditation clause is said ten times, beginning with the Lord's Prayer and ending with the Glory Be. The rosary beads can be used as a help in this form of meditation because the worshiper is relieved of the necessity of counting and can concentrate on the meditation itself.

In addition to meditations for Sundays and feast days, Dr. Herz has provided meditation suggestions for various aspects of spiritual life. By using these suggestions, the person praying can meditate on Christ as the way to the Father, the Beatitudes, patience in suffering, spiritual renewal, the relationship with God and many other special meditations that can fit into our life for times of joy, times of trial, times when the love of Christ and the need for him become uppermost in our minds.

In *My Words Are Spirit and Life,* Stephanie Herz presents a way to bring meditation back to the roots of our spiritual heritage, the Scriptures. By making the Scriptures the core of our meditation and prayer, we can make the message of the Mass for a particular Sunday or feast day more immediate by concentrating on specific biblical passages. *My Words Are Spirit and Life* is the ideal book to bring Christ and the Bible closer than ever before.

MY WORDS ARE SPIRIT
AND LIFE

MY WORDS ARE SPIRIT AND LIFE

Meeting Christ Through Daily Meditation

by Stephanie M. Herz, T.O.C.D.

IMAGE BOOKS
A Division of Doubleday & Company, Inc.
Garden City, New York
1979

ACKNOWLEDGMENTS

· The meditations from the Mass are taken from the Lectionary for Mass, Benziger, New York, 1970.

Bible texts from the Jerusalem Bible and used by permission of Doubleday & Company, Inc.

Meditation suggestions in the appendix, unless otherwise specified, are based on the Jerusalem Bible; *The Oxford Annotated Bible with the Apocrypha,* Revised Standard Version, Oxford University Press, copyrighted 1965; and translations from a German psalm book.

The quotations from the Vatican II Council are taken from *Documents of Vatican II,* American Press, New York, 1966. All rights reserved.

Interpretations of scriptures are taken from the *Jerome Biblical Commentary* by Raymond Brown, E.S.S., Joseph A. Fitzmeyer, S.J., and Roland Murphy, E. O. Carm., 1968; Prentice-Hall, Englewood Cliffs, New Jersey; and *A Catholic Commentary on Holy Scripture,* published by Nelson & Sons, Ltd., London and New York, 1952.

Guardini, Romano: *Prayer in Practice,* Pantheon Books, Inc., a division of Random House, Inc. New York. Copyright © 1957.

Guardini, Romano: *Das Jahr des Herrn,* Matthias-Gruenewald Verlag, Mainz, Germany, 2nd ed., 1955.

Guardini, Romano: *Der Herr,* Werkbund Verlag, Wuerzburg, 9th ed., 1951.

Guardini, Romano: *Theologische Gebete,* Joseph Knecht, Frankfurt a.M., 1944.

Jungmann, Joseph, S.J.: *The Good News, Yesterday and Today,* S. H. Sadlier, New York, 1962.

McNaspy, C. J., S.J., *Our Changing Liturgy,* Hawthorn Books, New York, 1966.

Pelikan, Jaroslav, ed.: *The Preaching of Chrysostom,* Fortress Press, Philadelphia, 1967. Copyright © 1967.

Rahner, Karl: *Spiritual Exercises,* 1965, Herder & Herder, New York.

Stuhlmueller, Carroll, C.P.: "Scriptural Depth" in: *Revival of the Liturgy,* Herder & Herder, New York, 1963.

CONTENTS

FOREWORD

Why yet another book on The Book? Hasn't everything already been said?

Yes and no. When the last book of the New Testament ended—apparently with the prayer "Come, Lord Jesus" and a blessing followed by a definitive "Amen"—God's final word had been said. But not the final word of our human response.

Yet even before the last word of the last book, the sacred co-authors themselves had begun to respond, to reflect. Psalmists reflect on the Pentateuch; Prophets on the awesome mystery of Abraham's call and the great Exodus; the later writings (the "Kethuvim") reflect on the entire Covenant.

Little wonder. Christians, for all their veneration of Holy Scripture, have never fancied that God had said everything at once; unlike the Moslem belief in God as sole author of the Koran, their vision is of God speaking "in many times and in many ways" ("polumerōs kai polutropōs"), as the author of the Epistle to the Hebrews puts it, perhaps echoing the author of Chronicles II, who sees God "tirelessly sending messenger after messenger."

True, the final message comes in "these last days," but we are still in precisely these last days, the eschatological moment. So it is that while looking forward, we are aware that God's word is as much present as it is past.

While our stance before God is that of recipients, in the posture of orants in the early catacomb art, with arms outstretched, we are not summoned to be like those who are without understanding. Our minds, no less than our ears and hearts, are gifts from God—gifts to be put to use.

Holy Scripture, then, is to be heard, to be lovingly received, but also to be reflected on. Prayerful discernment, based on ecclesial tradition and responsible scholarship but not stopping there, must go on if we are to grasp, to appropriate, what God is saying to us. To be merely passive may be the easy way, but it is hardly the right way. The better part chosen by Martha's sister Mary was not that of the spiritual vegetable. Really to hear Jesus involves more than somnolence.

This is not, I hope, said with the hubris of an intellectual deluded by love of learning or forgetful that Christ thanked his Father for opening the great mysteries to children. Scholarship cannot be an ultimate value, much less can mere sophistication or subtlety. In approaching Scripture we should be more at home on our knees than in the position of an entomologist peering at a bug. Exegesis, hermeneutics and their tools should be aids toward the simplicity and transparency and openness admired in the sort of children Christ seemed to have in mind. Blessed Claude de la Colombière literally read Scripture on his knees.

Happily we live at a time when Scripture is no longer used as a quarry for texts to be used controversially. Thanks to ecumenical collaboration, today we Catholics approach the Bible more comfortably, with no residue of the sort of bibliophobia that haunted some of our forebears in more defensive times.

Today we welcome Scheeben's view that Scripture "affords a fuller, deeper and more comprehensive understanding" of God's word. We see it, not in opposition to tradition, but as privileged and irreplaceable. In his profound work *Word and Revelation,* Urs von Balthasar suggests that since God's truth through Christ "is imparted to the soul in Scripture, no dialogue between God and the soul, however interior or mystical, ever takes precedence over Scripture or replaces it." The great mystics never denied or overlooked this core fact. One thinks immediately of Francis of Assisi, Ignatius of Loyola, Teresa of Ávila and Thérèse of Lisieux.

The problem remains: how best to approach Scripture? Experience suggests that the most obvious way—starting with Genesis and reading straight through, Deuteronomy and all—is seldom the most fruitful. One gets bogged down in tiny prescriptions that seem to bear little contemporary relevance.

Another way is simply to open the Bible at random, as though any text would prove applicable to any moment. Again experience seems not to find this best.

Stephanie Herz has found a better way, one based on the longer experience of Christian tradition. Years of personal meditation, following her rich encounter with Romano Guardini, finds the clue in the Church's own approach to Scripture. As Vatican Council II would put it, the faithful "should gladly put themselves in touch with the sacred text itself, whether it be through the liturgy, rich in the divine word, or through devotional reading," remembering "that prayer should accompany the reading of sacred Scripture, so that God and man may talk together" (*Constitution on Divine Revelation* No. 25).

The Bible is pre-eminently an ecclesial treasure, preserved by the Church, shared by members of the Church, especially in the living context of the liturgical year.

It was no surprise, then, that in the very first document passed by Vatican Council II, that on the sacred liturgy, the Church insisted that "in sacred celebrations there is to be more reading from holy Scripture, and it is to be more varied and suitable" (*Constitution on the Sacred Liturgy* No. 35:1). For while the liturgy does not exhaust the scope of Christian life, it must be central and other devotions should be related to it, grounded in the very word of God. "These devotions should be so drawn up that they harmonize with the liturgical seasons, accord with the sacred liturgy, are in some fashion derived from it, and lead the people to it, since the liturgy by its very nature far surpasses any of them" (ibid. No. 13).

The Council encourages Bible services and reminds us that we are also "to enter into our chamber to pray to the Father in secret" (ibid. Nos. 12 and 35). The present volume I find a great aid to both these practices.

While I suppose that Stephanie Herz did not design her book principally for priests and others involved in liturgical readings and homilies, I for one will find it a great help here, too.

Anyone who is to provide homilies day after day, or at least Sunday after Sunday, finds himself running out of fresh material. (In fact, I find this especially the case after publishing "Homily Hints" in the magazine *Aids in Ministry* for the three-year cycle.) The present volume will, I am confident, prove a stimulus to any priest fortunate enough to have it at hand.

We priests will be particularly helped by having homiletic material provided by one who is not an ordained priest. Stephanie Herz's reflections, while profoundly theological, are not "clerical" or written in "churchy" language. They may help us exorcise some of this from our preaching.

As an old friend of Fr. Joseph Jungmann and a student of many of his books, as well as those of Romano Guardini, I was especially happy to find a volume inspired by these liturgical giants. Doubtless they are both pleased to find a fresh flowering of their classic insights.

Rhythmic prayer, suggested in the techniques for meditation proposed here, has lately returned to popularity, perhaps inspired by mantras and other Eastern usages. Within the explicitly Christian tradition, the Jesus Prayer is being more and more used. Those in the Ignatian school like to point out the various styles proposed in the *Spiritual Exercises,* especially the "second method" (in which one dwells on sacred words "so long as he finds meanings, comparisons, relish, and consolation") and the "third method" ("at each breath saying one word of the Lord's Prayer or of any other that is being recited, so that only one word be said between each breath . . . in this rhythmical prayer").

This is not to say that Stephanie Herz's meditations are merely derivative or unoriginal. I mean to suggest only that they are rooted within a Christian freedom that allows the Spirit to breathe in a rich variety of ways.

C. J. McNaspy, S.J.
University Professor
Loyola University
New Orleans

INTRODUCTION

THE WORD OF GOD

Pascal has said: *"La philosophie est un sentiment du coeur."* Freely translated: "The philosophy we choose is a matter of the heart." Christ said: "Where your treasure is, there your heart will be" (Lk. 12:34). Similarly, the prayer or meditation we choose is one that fills or expresses our need of relating to God. This accounts for the fact that for many years I have used a form of meditating which in the light of recent publications on the liturgy is strictly Christocentric.

As far as I can think back we were taught in Germany: "Live with the Church." "Participate in the Mass." "Use the missal." The motto was: "Do not pray in the Mass, *pray the Mass*. Then go out and *live the Mass.*" Somewhat similar to Joergensen's statement that our life should be a continual Mass. At the public high school of Cologne, Germany, the Catholic chaplain talked to the Catholic students the day before the monthly Communion Sunday by way of interpreting the meaning of the Mass of the next day. He suggested that we meditate every Saturday evening on the gospel of the Sunday in order that "we would enter into the spirit of the particular Mass." During my student days at the University of Berlin, when I lived in a Catholic residence for students, the chaplain held a short service every night in the chapel, during which he laid out the points for meditation on the liturgy of the next morning. Personal acquaintance with Fr. Romano Guardini whose courses and seminar at the University of Berlin I attended helped to develop meditation.

In time I adopted a special method and jotted down my meditations so that I could improve on them as they recurred over the years. By a strange accident they were discovered recently by a priest. He commented: "This is exactly the kind of prayer we need for our time." After having tested them out with his confreres, he recommended that I get them ready for publication. That is how my card file of three-by-fives was "updated" into a more permanent form.

The meditations in this book are based on the Vatican II "Liturgy of the Word." By liturgy is meant the public and official act of worship of the Church. The Constitution on the Liturgy of Vatican II says: "Every liturgical celebration is an action of Christ the priest and of His body the Church."[1]

The liturgy was changed considerably by the Vatican II Council. The renewal initiated has to be seen as a culminating point of all the efforts of the preceding sixty years to revitalize the liturgy and make it an enlivening force in the spirituality of the faithful. The fact that the Holy Spirit blew the schema on the Liturgy right on top of the agenda of the Church Fathers, and that he changed the course of the Rhine so that it "flowed into the Tiber,"[2] makes it quite evident that the Holy Spirit was very much alive and active in promoting the "updating" of the Church.

The goal of the Vatican II Council on the liturgy was to renew ourselves, to bring a deeper penetration of the faithful by the Word of God and the Christian doctrine, and thereby to make us ever more faithful witnesses of Christ.

The guidelines for this renewal were: to make revisions in

[1] *Documents of Vatican II,* America Press, New York, p. 141. Copyright © 1966.

[2] For details see Ralph Wiltgen, S.V.D., *The Rhine Flows into the Tiber,* Hawthorn Books, New York, 1967, pp. 19–24, 1st edition.

the light of sound tradition; to make changes in the rites so that they may be given new vigor to meet the circumstances and needs of modern times. The Constitution also spells out the principle of continuing change in the future, so that it will remain open or "living" as characterized by Father Kilian McDonnell, O.S.B., in his article on Calvin's conception of the liturgy.[3] By remaining flexible, it will avoid calcification, which any society must avoid if it wants to survive.

Safeguarding sound tradition and using what is pertinent for our days means studying the tradition of the ancient past and the liturgy throughout the ages, going back to the roots of our spiritual heritage. Fortunately, a great deal of research on the liturgy had preceded Vatican II. Many forerunners of reform of the liturgy had made valuable contributions. These made possible the outstanding changes which Vatican II has given us. Tributaries from other fields came from the Catholic Action movement to which the popes have called the laity beginning with the call of Pope Pius IX on September 25, 1876. Another one is the social action movement which in Germany was led by Bishop Von Ketteler of Mainz. His social action program was taken over in full by Pope Leo XIII in *Rerum Novarum*.

Of the many scholars on the liturgy I like to concentrate first on Fr. Joseph Andreas Jungmann, S.J., because in my estimation he was one of the most influential pre-Vatican II liturgists. The essence of Jungmann's contribution can be summarized—leaving out all the details—under five headings: What to teach? How to teach? In what spirit? What is the goal? What should be the result?

The content of Christian teaching should be Christ, Christ the Saviour, the whole Christ as the Church presents him throughout the Church year. The content should bring before the faithful the vision of God's great plan of salvation, as presented in Ephesians 1:3-23, and in many other letters of St. Paul where he tells us that the Father has given us every blessing in heaven through Christ and in Christ, through Christ's

[3] Published in: *The Crisis of Liturgical Reform*, Concilium Vol. 42, Paulist Fathers, 1969, p. 93.

blood, that the Father has put all things under Christ our leader and our King. Christ is the center to which we must gravitate. Nothing but a Christocentric religion can redeem us and free us from ourselves and lead us to God. Christ calls us to follow him, Christ wants to live in us, Christ wants to be resurrected in us. We should become other Christs, restore all things in Christ, so that the whole creation participates in the harmony of the love of the Father and the brotherhood of men which Beethoven has glorified in his Ninth Symphony.

How to teach? Christ, the teacher, himself has shown the way: When he joined two of his disciples on the road to Emmaus, he interpreted the Scriptures to them, since they had not grasped the meaning of the prophets in relation to him. Later, the disciples said that their hearts were burning inside them when he talked to them. Why? The message of redemption by the Father's plan of salvation is the most joyous message. There is nothing in the world that could give us greater joy than the message of salvation, the message that he is *eternal life*. "My words are spirit and life" (Jn. 6:63). But this message has to be presented so that the meaning of Christ's coming reaches our hearts and our wills, not just the intellect. The way to teach Christ is to make him come alive in everybody of the community of the faithful. The Acts say that after the descent of the Holy Spirit at Pentecost the apostles were filled with the Spirit and thus were able to pass on his Spirit to their listeners. They taught Christ as they had experienced him, as they had walked with him, and had listened to his teaching. They had seen his compassionate love for the suffering, the lame, the sick, the blind and the poor. They had seen his merciful forgiving attitude toward sinners. They finally understood the mysteries of his suffering, death and resurrection: the nucleus of our redemption. After meeting him repeatedly after his resurrection, they could say with the greatest joy: "He lives!" Their message was absolutely Christ-centered. The way of teaching Christ must be a joyous proclamation of the Good News of our redemption, a kerygmatic message. The right way of teaching Christ should

lead to the formation of the mature Christian and his commit-
ment.

The spirit in which to teach the gospel should be by and
through the Spirit of Christ: "The zeal for your house con-
sumes me" (Jn. 2:17). "I have come to light a fire on earth"
(Lk. 12:49). St. Paul says in 1 Corinthians 2:4–5: "My message and my preaching had none of the persuasive force of 'wise'
argumentation, but the convincing power of the spirit. As a
consequence your faith rests not on the wisdom of men, but on
the power of God." Paul was filled with the Spirit of Christ:
"The love of Christ impels me" (2 Cor. 5:14). The teaching
done in the Spirit of Christ cannot help but have a very dynamic
effect on the community of the faithful, in fact on every individual who has responded to Christ's: "Be thou open!"

Jungmann saw as the goal of preaching: to proclaim the
sacred message of redemption "as clearly and intelligibly as
possible to impart knowledge." Knowledge of redemption should
lead to the appreciation of the great value of our redemption
and arouse in the faithful the desire to follow him. The goal is
to form the mature Christian who takes his place in the Mystical
Body of Christ. Both St. Paul and St. John have stressed the
importance of giving the right kind of knowledge.

The result of the first four points will be that man will will-
ingly and joyously embrace his share in the Divine plan of salvation, grow into spiritual maturity and participate in the redemp-
tive work of Christ, and work for "the building up of the Body
of Christ" (Eph. 4:12).

Jungmann's ideas and philosophy found a very good echo in
the Vatican II Constitution on the Liturgy, especially in the
"Liturgy of the Word." This new name which the Church Fathers gave to the scriptural part of the Mass indicates the emphasis that they put on the use of the Scriptures in the worship
of God and sanctification of man. In apostolic times it was called
the Mass of the Catechumen who received instruction in the
faith. Later centuries called it the scriptural part, but the importance of the Word of God was lost, somehow. What the
Church Fathers did at Vatican II was to "reestablish balance,

to restore proportions in our worship."[4] It was necessary to stress the significance of God's Word in our life and in our worship. If to be a Christian means to have the Spirit of Christ, then we will find him in the Scriptures. Pope John XXIII had spoken in the opening address of Vatican II about "the step forward toward a doctrinal penetration."[5] To achieve this, the Constitution on the Liturgy arranged for a "richer fare by opening up the treasures of the Bible more lavishly."[6] The Sunday readings of the Mass were increased to three, a psalm was added. A homily should be given to the faithful every Sunday, which is to be based on the text of the Scriptures. The homily is considered part of the Word of God, since the priest in his official capacity expounds the mysteries of faith and moral doctrine in the place of Christ. Moreover, the Scripture readings are drawn from a much wider range of the Bible than in the past, the readings varying over a cycle of three years: Jungmann's idea of providing the right kind of knowledge to nourish our faith. With the wider range of the readings we get a better and fuller picture of Christ and his spirit. More Scripture readings, if properly assimilated, might create greater intensity of Christ's life in us.

Of the greatest importance is the way that the word and the homily are to be presented. The Constitution on the Liturgy speaks of a "proclamation" of the Word in Section Six and repeats this many times. Proclamation to St. John was: "What we have seen and heard we proclaim to you so that you may share life with us" (1 Jn. 1:3). If proclamation is witnessing to what we have seen and heard, then the proclaimer must be inspired and filled with the mystery of God's love and Christ's great salvific work. Footnote 20 of Section Fourteen of the Constitution on the Liturgy says *in small print* that "priests and future priests are required to become deeply imbued with litur-

[4] McNaspy, C. J., S.J., *Our Changing Liturgy,* Hawthorn Books, New York, 1966, p. 65.

[5] *Documents of Vatican II,* America Press, New York, copyright © 1966, p. 715.

[6] Ibid., p. 155.

gical spirit."[7] Proclamation means to speak in such a way that *Christ becomes alive* when the Scriptures are read.

Carroll Stuhlmueller, C.P., like some others, points out that in the Old Testament Scriptural readings were not historical events, but a reliving of the past: "They were to be experienced as vital forces."[8] The messages were to become actualized for the present day. For the apostles this actualization was made possible through the gift of the Holy Spirit at Pentecost. By the way they presented Christ the events and words of Jesus became living realities. By the way the gospel is proclaimed today, Christ becomes a reality in our days. The liturgy of the Word then becomes a prayerful reliving of Christ. The inspired proclaimer of the "Word" will inspire and arouse in the faithful the desire to follow Christ. The liturgy of the Word will glorify God at the same time that it sanctifies man. Perhaps a well-known saying of Goethe that has become proverbial in Germany might fit in here: "You will not reach heart to heart, unless it is coming from your heart."[9]

As a sociologist I can only recommend that more use be made of the wealth of sound principles of sociology that we find throughout the Old and the New Testaments. If we want people to become properly socialized in the Divine Community, it would not hurt to stress the principle that "grace builds on nature," if we hope to counteract and overcome the egocentrism of our day by a Christocentric attitude.

The Church Fathers point out in Section Twelve of the Constitution on the Liturgy that the Christian "must also enter into his chamber to pray to the Father in secret."[10] The Constitution on the Revelation of Vatican II recommends the prayerful reading of the Scriptures "so that we may hope for a new surge of

[7] Ibid., p. 144.

[8] Carroll Stuhlmueller, C.P., "Scriptural Liturgical Depth," in: *The Revival of the Liturgy,* Herder & Herder, 1963, p. 20.

[9] Goethe, *Faust,* Inselverlag, Leipzig, Germany, p. 150.

[10] *Documents of Vatican II,* America Press, New York, copyright © 1966, p. 143.

spiritual vitality from intensified veneration for God's word."[11] The Dogmatic Constitution on the Church spells out the principle of full-fledged citizenship of the laity: "In a special way the priesthood of the laity is a participation in the priesthood of Christ."[12] The Church offers us in the Bible all the wealth that we can ask for. It is a great wealth indeed. But it has to be internalized. There is a way to do that. "What you have inherited from your ancestors, you have to acquire it, in order to make it your own."[13] Maturity in the spiritual life would mean that we are responsible and take the initiative on our own, to acquire the spiritual wealth that we have inherited from our ancestors. One way of doing that is by way of meditation.

[11] Ibid., p. 128.
[12] Ibid., p. 27.
[13] Goethe, *Faust,* Inselverlag, Leipzig, p. 152.

METHODS AND FORMS OF PRAYER

෨

Meditating is a special way of praying. Prayer has been defined by theologians as a raising of the mind to God. It means a reverent speaking to God in the awareness of his holiness and almighty power. The way to do this is "to free oneself of everything which is irrelevant, and to hold oneself at the disposal of God who alone matters now."[14] "If he wants to pray he must recall himself from everything and everywhere and become and remain present."[15] It means to center all our powers on God alone to the exclusion of everything else. This is possible only by the grace of the Holy Spirit. "Without me you can do nothing" (Jn. 15:5).

Every prayer can become a renewal in God if we ask the Father in the name of Christ, as he taught us to do in the last discourse with his apostles. In prayer we should abide in Christ. In fact, we should abide in him at all times. Pray unceasingly! (1 Thess. 5:17). In his farewell address Christ asked his apostles again and again to abide in him as he abides in the Father (Jn. 15:4). The highest form of prayer is adoration and praise of God. Christ gave it the first place when he taught the apostles the Our Father. Petitions for our spiritual and temporal needs should take secondary place. Christ stated that our prayers of petition should be made always in his name. "Anything that you ask in my name, I will do" (Jn. 14:14).

There are various methods of praying. Vocal prayer uses the

[14] Guardini, Romano, *Prayer in Practice,* Pantheon Books, New York, p. 13.

[15] Ibid., p. 14.

spoken word; meditation, in general, uses less of the spoken word, but means to think about, to dwell on some phase of the Divine truth, on Christ, on some event of his life, and on the mysteries of salvation. In meditating we are to use all our powers of mind, soul, understanding, testing, imagination: to get images of hope, feelings, will, and heart.

Depending on the emphasis, the method of meditation varies: Some stress more the understanding, others the affective faculties. But all are to apply the will. There are also degrees of intensity in meditation, which are related to the time spent in meditating, or the repetition of meditating on the same subject by which the content penetrates more deeply.

It is possible also to combine vocal prayer with the meditation by way of repetition. I have adopted this method of meditating from Romano Guardini. He developed and presented it in his meditations: *The Year of the Lord*.[16] These meditations are based on the Mass of Trent. Guardini wrote this book right after his masterpiece *The Lord*. After he had presented in *The Lord* the new way of living in Christ, he wanted to open up the concept of the Way, the Truth, and the Life for prayer. He wanted to help modern man to encounter Christ *in prayer,* the liturgy of the Mass to become a private prayerful reliving of Christ.

In his unique method Guardini was ahead of his time. His method fits the needs of modern man and his restlessness. It is Christocentric and leads us directly to Christ in prayer. I had used Guardini's *Year of the Lord* for many years when Vatican II made it somewhat obsolete, because of the fundamental revision of the Liturgy of the Word. Guardini's method, however, proved to be of timeless value. In fact, it fits perfectly with the pastoral attitude of Vatican II which stresses Christ and his work in the Divine plan of salvation. To "live with the Church" and remain up-to-date I started to make my own medi-

---

[16] Guardini, Romano, *Das Jahr des Herrn,* Matthias-Gruenewald Verlag, Mainz, 1953, 2nd ed.

tations on the new Liturgy of the Word. I continued to use Guardini's ingenious method of meditating and his meditation frame.

Meditation Frame: Text, Components, and Form

The meditation frame used in this book has been literally translated from Romano Guardini's book *The Year of the Lord*. The first part reads:

> Praised be the Lord, the holy and mighty,
> The Son of the living God, who . . .

The second part reads:

> Jesus Christ, Saviour of the world,
> Our master and our brother,
> Have mercy on us"[17]

except for Good Friday when the petition is taken from the Good Friday liturgy and reads:

> Holy is God!
> Holy and strong!
> Holy Immortal One!
> Have mercy on us!

For worshipers who desire a longer petition, Guardini suggested another version:

> Jesus Christ, Saviour of the world, lead us the good way,
> and after our death be a merciful judge to us.

All the components of the meditation frame can be found in the New Testament. The frame also contains the Jesus prayer of the Eastern rites of the Church which reads: "Jesus Christ, Son of the Living God, have mercy on us." Guardini stated in his book that he toiled long and for many years to find a satis-

[17] Ibid., pp. 26–27.

factory but simplified method which made it possible to meditate even under unfavorable circumstances. He did not reveal, however, any special sources which he might have used. There is a possibility that he might have built his meditation frame on the apostolic creed of the first centuries, because the attributes of the Three Divine persons given in the apostolic creed are the major components of his meditation frame: *"Almighty, Holy, Jesus Christ, Son of God, Our Lord, Saviour."*[18]

With regard to the form of prayer used in the meditation frame we find in the first part adoration pure and total. We praise Christ, his holiness, his almighty power, his divinity by addressing him as the Son of the Living God. It is the highest form of praying. The second part is a petition in which we ask the Saviour of the world to have mercy on us. By asking in his name we draw his power into our heart and our soul.

Nature of Meditations Suggested in this Book

Every meditation in this book is addressed to Christ. The approach is totally Christocentric: to make Christ the center of our life, of our thinking, of our feeling, and of our acting.

By having a meditation frame that is addressed to Christ, and the meditation focused on Christ, they reinforce each other. When we praise God directly in the opening invocation, our mind is elevated to him, our hearts are opened to him and made receptive for the food of the Word of God, which follows. By invoking the name of Jesus in the petition, and asking for his mercy, we draw his power into our hearts. Our spiritual life and our relationship with God are strengthened. The life of God is deepened in our soul. "Dwelling for a while in the presence of God in meditation is in itself a holy and salutary event which may effect us profoundly. Meditation thus becomes an encounter between God and man. For whenever we apprehend

[18] Fr. Jungmann quotes these attributes in his *Good News Yesterday and Today,* Ch. 3, S. H. Sadlier, New York, 1962.

some particular trait of his holy character or appreciate the meaning of one of his sayings, our mind is enriched."[19]

How to Make the Meditation and Use the Book

The basic unit of the meditation consists of the praise of God in the invocation, plus the meditation proper plus the petition. For example: If we take the first meditation of second Sunday of Advent of the A-year, the first meditation looks like this:

> PRAISED BE THE LORD, THE HOLY AND MIGHTY,
> THE SON OF THE LIVING GOD,
> WHOSE COMING ILLUMINATES OUR DARKNESS,
> JESUS CHRIST, SAVIOUR OF THE WORLD,
> OUR MASTER AND OUR BROTHER, HAVE MERCY ON US.

This is the essence of the prayer. It is repeated ten times in order to develop it. Each meditation is opened by one Our Father and concluded with a Glory be to the Father, and to the Son and to the Holy Spirit, as it was in the beginning, is now and will be forever. Amen.

Graphically the structure of the whole prayer looks like this:

One   Our Father

SAY
TEN
TIMES
{
PRAISED BE THE LORD, THE HOLY AND MIGHTY,

THE SON OF THE LIVING GOD, WHO

INSERT MEDITATION CLAUSE . . .

JESUS CHRIST, SAVIOUR OF THE WORLD,

OUR MASTER AND OUR BROTHER, HAVE

MERCY ON US.

Glory Be . . .

[19] Guardini, Romano, *Prayer in Practice,* Pantheon Books, New York, 1957, p. 145.

Repeat the above for each of the five meditations that are prepared for each Sunday. The structure of the prayer and the meditation frame are given on the last printed sheet of this book, one side giving the structure, the other side the meditation frames which can be varied. You can cut out this sheet and laminate or cover with transparent tape to make it more durable. The use of rosary beads is recommended as a real help in saying the meditations. The worshiper is relieved of the necessity of counting and can concentrate on the meditation. It also will accentuate the rhythm of the prayer.

The meditation is developed by saying it slowly, abiding with Christ, staying with him, so that the event or mystery we meditate on becomes alive in us. Meditation is the prayerful reliving of the life of Christ.

The meditations are based on the Liturgy of the Word of Vatican II. Following Guardini's pattern I have selected five events of Christ's life from each Sunday of the Church year for the three-year cycle and for the Solemnities of the Lord during the season of the year. Since Vatican II the years are marked A, B, C in rotation. 1975 was an A-year, 1976 a B-year, 1977 a C-year. 1978 starts the cycle anew as an A-year. Most Sundays have their own Mass each year: consequently the meditations for the A-year are marked A, for the B-year marked B, for the C-year marked C. You will find the letter A or B or C opposite the meditation in the liturgical part when you have a different Mass for each Sunday of the three-year cycle. For the great high feast days, where the Masses remain the same for the three years, initials are omitted completely: see Vigil of Christmas, the three Masses of Christmas, January 1st, and others. Because the wealth on the high feast days, however, is so great, three sets of meditations have been prepared, and they are marked I, I, and III. You may take one set, or two, or all three.

In formulating the meditation phrases I have tried to stay as close as possible to the wording of the Scriptures. When interpretations or abbreviations are used, they are based on the text of the Liturgy of the Word and three additional sources: Guardini's book *The Lord,* the *Catholic Commentary on Holy Scriptures,* published by Thomas Nelson, 1953, New York; and the *Jerome Biblical Commentary* edited by Raymond Brown, S.S., Joseph Fitzmeyer, S.J., and Roland Murphy, O.Carm., Prentice-Hall, 1968, Englewood Cliffs, New Jersey. With all this help there remained difficulties. If they were met halfway, it is due to the linguistic mastership and sculptured brevity of expression of the commentators of the *Jerome Biblical Commentary* which made it possible to cast the material into the given meditation frame and relate it to Christ in a rhythmic way.

The passage from which the meditation is taken in the Liturgy of the Word is indicated at the bottom of the meditation set when only one source was used. When more than one source has been used, no annotations are given. No annotation is given either in cases of free interpretation of the Mass.

The meditation suggestions are but an extract, so to speak, of the Scriptures, because they had to be kept short. They bring the highlights, but not the details. For a full understanding the worshiper does well to read the biblical-liturgical text of the liturgy as given in the annotation. Thereby the meditation will become more meaningful and alive.

The Sunday meditations can be used on the weekdays following Sunday. In the appendix the reader will find additional meditations. Instructions about their use are given on the first page of the appendix.

In using this form of meditating, the worshiper does well to give the meditation adequate time. The meaning of meditating is to abide, to encounter Christ prayerfully, in an attentive way, in inner quiet and alertness, in the conscious presence of God, and to surrender to his truth as presented. The goal is to relive Christ prayerfully through his life, and through his word, so as to praise him, to petition him, and to abide in him.

Eventually and hopefully, the reader will make this method his own, so that he will develop his own meditations. That might be done from the Liturgy of the Word of the weekdays of the

Church year, from the Scriptures, or from books of spiritual reading. He will select those passages which have touched him. By meditating on them he will incorporate them into his spiritual life. The essence of Christian existence is encounter with Christ. These meditations are offered to facilitate this encounter.

MEDITATION SUGGESTIONS

from the

THREE-YEAR LECTIONARY CYCLE OF VATICAN II SUNDAY AND HOLIDAY MASSES

PROPER OF SEASONS

ADVENT SEASON

FIRST SUNDAY OF ADVENT

A 1   Whose temple shall tower above the mountains.

2   To whose house all nations shall stream.

3   Who will establish eternal peace.

4   Who warns us to put on the armor of light.

5   Who asks us to be awake until he comes.

B 1   Whose coming we desire with longing hearts.

2   Who will redeem us from our sins.

3   For whose revelation we are waiting eagerly.

4   Who will steady us to the end.

5   Who warned us to be awake.

C 1   Whom signs precede in the heavens.

2   Who comes in a cloud with power and great majesty.

3   Who gives the just cause to rejoice.

4   Whose coming will be sudden.

5   Who warned us to be ready at all times.

[Lk. 21:25–36]

SECOND SUNDAY OF ADVENT

A 1 Whose coming illuminates our darkness.

2 Who was prophesied by Isaiah.

3 Whose way was prepared by John.

4 Whose paths we should make straight.

5 Who will baptize with the Holy Spirit and fire.

B 1 Whose messenger prepared the way of the Lord.

2 For whom every valley shall be filled.

3 For whom every mountain shall be laid low.

4 Whose glory shall be revealed.

5 Who will feed his flock like a shepherd.

[Is. 40:1–5; 9–11]

C 1 Whom John proclaimed by Isaiah's prophecy.

2 Whose path we should make straight.

3 For whom every valley shall be filled.

4 For whom every mountain shall be leveled.

5 Whose salvation all mankind shall see.

[Lk. 3:1–6]

THIRD SUNDAY OF ADVENT

A 1 Whose coming brings great joy.

2 After whom we need not wait for another.

3 . Who heals the blind and the deaf.

4 Who brings Good News to the poor.

5 Who blessed the man of faith.

[Mt. 11:2–11]

B 1 To whom is given the Spirit of the Lord.

2 Who is the anointed one of God.

3 Who brings the Good News to the poor.

4 To whom John witnessed as the light.

5 Whose way was prepared by John.

C 1 In whom we should rejoice always.

2 Whose coming should remove all fear.

3 Who is right in our midst.

4 Whose coming was prepared by the Baptist.

5 Whose baptism in the Holy Spirit was predicted by John.

FOURTH SUNDAY OF ADVENT

A 1 Whose Mother was with child by the Holy Spirit.

2 Whose foster father considered to divorce her quietly.

3 Whose angel revealed to Joseph the mystery of Christ's conception.

4 Whose angel removed Joseph's concern.

5 Whose birth by a virgin had been foretold by Isaiah.

[Mt. 1:18–24]

B 1 Whose coming was revealed by an angel.

2 Whose angel announced to Mary God's plan of salvation.

3 Whose plan first deeply troubled Mary.

4 Whose angel reassured Mary: "The Holy Spirit will come upon you."

5 To whom Mary submitted: "Let his will be done!"

[Lk. 1:26–38]

C 1 Whom the clouds may rain down.

2 Whom the earth may bring forth.

3 For whom God prepared a body.

4 Who came to do God's will.

5 Through whose body we have been redeemed once for all.

CHRISTMAS SEASON

CHRISTMAS VIGIL: AFTERNOON OF DECEMBER 24TH

1   Who is coming to save us.

2   Whose glory we shall see in the morning.

3   Whose birth marks the beginning of our redemption.

4   Whose name is Emmanuel: God with us.

5   Whose glory shall be revealed to all mankind.

CHRISTMAS: MASS AT MIDNIGHT

1   To whom God said: "You are my Son. This day I have begotten you."

2   Whom Mary had conceived by the Holy Spirit.

3   To whom she gave birth during Holy Night.

4   In whom God's grace was revealed to us.

5   Whose birth the angels announced to the shepherds.

[Lk. 2:1–14]

CHRISTMAS: MASS AT DAWN

1   Whose glory the angels announced.

2   Who gives us his peace and his grace.

3   Whose kindness and love appeared to save us.

4   Whom the shepherds adored in the manger.

5   Whose mother treasured and reflected on all these things.

CHRISTMAS: MASS AT DAYTIME

1   Who had no beginnings but is from eternity.

2   Who is the true light that enlightens all men.

3   Through whom all things were made.

4   Who empowered all who accept him to become children of God.

5   From whose fullness we have all received.

[Jn. 1:1–18]

SUNDAY IN THE OCTAVE OF CHRISTMAS, HOLY FAMILY

A 1 Whom the Father sent when all was ready.

2 Whom the shepherds found in the manger.

3 Who gave us an example of humility and meekness.

4 Through whom we give thanks to the Father.

5 Whose peace may rule in our hearts and families.

B 1 Whose parents took him to the temple.

2 Whom Simeon greeted as the salvation of God.

3 Who is destined for the fall and rising of many.

4 Who is destined to be a sign of rejection.

5 By whom many hearts will be revealed.

[Lk. 2:22–40]

C 1 Who stayed behind in his "Father's house."

2 Whose parents did not understand.

3 Who returned with them to Nazareth.

4 Who was subject to them.

5 Who grew in age, wisdom, and grace.

[Lk. 2:41–52]

JANUARY 1ST OCTAVE OF CHRISTMAS, SOLEMNITY OF MARY, MOTHER OF GOD

1 Who was born by the Virgin Mary.

2 Who regarded the humility of his handmaid.

3 Who has done great things to Mary.

4 Whose mother was wholly united to him.

5 Who gave us his mother at Calvary.

[Lk. 2:16–21]

SECOND SUNDAY AFTER CHRISTMAS

1 Who has blessed us with all spiritual blessings.

2 Who chose us before the world was made.

3 Through whom we have become God's adopted sons.

4 Who was present to God in the beginning.

5 Who became flesh and dwelt among us.

JANUARY 6TH—EPIPHANY

I

1 Who was revealed by the guidance of a star.

2 To whom the Wise Men came to adore him.

3 To whom they brought royal gifts.

4 Whose glory appeared to all nations.

5 By whose light all nations shall walk.

II

1 Who is the ruler of the universe.

2 To whom belong the kingship, the government, and the power.

3 Who rules mysteriously over the hearts of men.

4 To whom all mankind will be subject.

5 Who leads us to glory by faith.

III

1 Through whose epiphany our redemption becomes reality.

2 Who is the sacrifice that reconciles us to the Father.

3 Who is our Saviour and Redeemer.

4 Whose star is our guide to eternal life.

5 Who forms us into his image.

SUNDAY AFTER JANUARY 6TH—
BAPTISM OF THE LORD

A 1 Who is the chosen one of God.

2 Whom the Father endowed with his Spirit.

3 Who, in humility, requested baptism from John.

4 Who did all "that righteousness demands."

5 Whose baptism revealed the mystery of the Trinity.

B 1 Who was baptized by John in the Jordan.

2 To whom the Father witnessed as his beloved Son.

3 Upon whom the Spirit descended like a dove.

4 Whose baptism revealed the mystery of the Trinity.

5 Who is the covenant and light to all nations.

C 1 Whose forerunner baptized with water.

2 Whose sandal straps John felt unfit to loosen.

3 On whom the Spirit descended like a dove.

4 Whose mission was approved by his Father's voice.

5 Whose baptism revealed the mystery of the Trinity.

[Lk. 3:15–16; 21–22]

LENTEN SEASON

❧

FIRST SUNDAY OF LENT

A 1 Who was led by the Spirit into the wilderness.

2 Who fasted forty days.

3 Who was tempted by Satan three times.

4 On whom the temptations came to naught.

5 Who taught us to reject all evil-doing.

[Mt. 4:1–11]

B 1 Who was put to the test by Satan.

2 On whom the angels waited.

3 Who calls us to reform our lives.

4 Who came to lead us to God.

5 Who saved us by a baptismal bath.

C 1 Who calls us to fast and self-denial.

2 Who taught us to reject all evil-doing.

3 Who rescues all who cling to him.

4 Who answers everyone who invokes him.

5 Who saves everyone who calls on his name.

SECOND SUNDAY OF LENT

A　1　Who led Peter, James, and John up a high mountain.

　　2　Who was transfigured in their presence.

　　3　Who spoke with Moses and Elijah.

　　4　Whose Father testified in his behalf.

　　5　Whose face my heart does seek.

[Mt. 17:1–9]

B　1　Who revealed his glory to his apostles.

　　2　Who reveals himself to his faithful.

　　3　Who reveals his glory in the mysteries of the Church.

　　4　Who reveals himself to the little ones.

　　5　Whose transfiguration anticipates our own.

C　1　Who calls us to bear our share of hardship.

　　2　Who has called us to a life of holiness.

　　3　Whose appearance made manifest the Divine glory.

　　4　Who has robbed death of its power.

　　5　Whose disciple must ascend Calvary with him.

THIRD SUNDAY OF LENT

A 1   Who was thirsty for the faith of the Samaritan woman.

  2   Who asked her for water to drink.

  3   Who awakened her desire for faith.

  4   Who has living water that lasts for all eternity.

  5   Whose food is to do the will of the Father.

[Jn. 4:5–42]

B 1   Who found the Temple desecrated into a market place.

  2   Who drove the merchants out from the Temple.

  3   Whom the Jews asked for a sign.

  4   Who said: "Destroy this temple, and I shall rebuild it in three days."

  5   Who "did not trust them because he knew them all."

[Jn. 2:13–25]

C 1   Who warns us to watch lest we fall.

  2   Who does not wish the sinner to die.

  3   Who told them to reform, the Kingdom was at hand.

  4   Who told them the parable of the unproductive fig tree.

  5   Who warns that we must bear fruit.

[Lk. 13:1–9]

FOURTH SUNDAY OF LENT

A 1 Who felt called by the man born blind.

2 Who cured him from his blindness.

3 Whose miracle is a sign of light Divine.

4 Whom the Pharisees rejected in spiritual blindness.

5 Who "came to make the sightless see, and the seeing blind."

[Jn. 9:1–41]

B 1 Who must be lifted up to draw all men.

2 Who was sent by the Father's love.

3 Who came into the world to bring eternal life.

4 Who calls us into the light from darkness.

5 Who is the Truth that sets us free.

[Jn. 3:14–21]

C 1 Who told about the prodigal who squandered his inheritance.

2 Who told about the prodigal's change of heart.

3 Who told about his decision to return home and ask his father's forgiveness.

4 Who said that his father ran to meet him and feast him.

5 Whose Father rejoiced because his son had been dead and had come back to life.

[Lk. 15:11–32]

FIFTH SUNDAY OF LENT

A 1 Who wept in compassion over the death of Lazarus.

2 Who raised Lazarus from the dead.

3 Who is the resurrection and the life.

4 Who will not let us die if we believe in him.

5 Who underwent death, so that we have life eternal.

[Jn. 11:1–45]

B 1 With whom we must die to be reborn.

2 Whom we must follow if we would serve him.

3 Whose Father will honor anyone who serves him.

4 Whose hour of glorification had come.

5 Who will draw all men to himself—once lifted up.

[Jn. 12:20–33]

C 1 To whom they brought a woman caught in adultery.

2 Who started writing on the ground.

3 Who said: "The one without sin cast the first stone."

4 Who was left alone with her after they all departed.

5 Who did not condemn her, but told her, "Sin no more."

[Jn. 8:1–11]

PASSION SUNDAY—PALM SUNDAY

I

1 Who entered Jerusalem as the King of Glory.

2 Who is of the royal House of David.

3 On whose road they spread their cloaks.

4 Whom they greeted with palm branches.

5 To whom they cried: "Hosanna to the Son of David!"

II

1 Who suffered the agony of body and soul.

2 Who was betrayed by Judas.

3 Who was condemned as a blasphemer.

4 Who was abandoned by God and men.

5 Who was crucified for our sins.

III

1 Who carried his Passion into glory.

2 Whose face will behold us for all eternity.

3 Whose defeat is the victory of God.

4 Who redeemed us by his suffering and death.

5 Who calls us to continue his sacrifice in our lives.

[Mt. 21: 1–11; 27:11–54]
[Mk. 11: 1–10; 15: 1–39]
[Lk. 19:28–40; 23: 1–49]

HOLY THURSDAY—MASS OF THE LORD'S SUPPER

I

1 Who offered an unbloody true sacrifice at the Last Supper.
2 Who gave them his body and blood for life everlasting.
3 Whose Eucharist makes us all one body.
4 Who gave us a memorial for all times.
5 Whose Eucharist is the eternal call of God's love.

[1 Cor. 11:23–26]

II

1 Who prepared to return to the Father.
2 Who loved his own to the end.
3 Who washed the feet of his disciples.
4 Who gave us an example of humility.
5 Who gave them a new commandment: "Love one another."

[Jn. 13:1–15]

III

1 Who went to Gethsemane to do his Father's will.
2 Whose soul was sorrowful unto death.
3 Whose sweat became drops of blood.
4 Who felt the crushing weight of all our sins.
5 Who made a complete surrender to God's will.

GOOD FRIDAY[1]—PASSION OF OUR LORD

I

1   Who became despised and rejected by men.
2   Who became a man of sorrows and familiar with suffering.
3   Who was pierced through for our faults.
4   Through whose wounds we are healed.
5   Who was led to the slaughter like a Lamb never opening its mouth.

[Is. 52:13–53:12]

II

1   Who was betrayed by Judas, abandoned by his apostles.
2   Whom the Sanhedrin had condemned before he testified.
3   Who, being God, was accused of blasphemy.
4   Whom they accused of rebellion before Pilate.
5   Whom Pilate found guiltless and condemned to crucifixion.

[Jn. 18:1–19:42]

III

1   Who was crucified with criminals.
2   Whose Mother stood at the foot of the Cross.
3   Who took the sins of the whole world upon himself.
4   Who was completely abandoned by his Father.
5   Who completed his mission and died.

[Jn. 18:1–19:42]

[1] The petition prayer for Good Friday is taken from the Liturgy as follows: "Holy is God! Holy and strong. Holy Immortal One, Have mercy on us!"

EASTER:
THE RESURRECTION OF THE LORD

EASTER VIGIL

I

1   Who is the light of the world.

2   Who is the Alpha and Omega.

3   Who broke the chains of death.

4   Who rose triumphantly from the grave.

5   Who reconciled us with God.

II

1   Who is risen, allelujah!

2   Who has ransomed us with his blood.

3   Who is the true Lamb that was slain.

4   With whom we are united in his death and resurrection.

5   Who is the high priest of the new covenant.

III

1   Who is the light that illuminates every man.

2   In whose death we are buried.

3   Through whose resurrection we receive new life.

4   Who is my Saviour, my courage, and my strength.

5   Who gives us his peace.

EASTER SUNDAY

I

1   Who conquered the power of death.

2   Who opened the way to eternal life.

3   Who is our eternal mediator and high priest.

4   With whom we have been raised from death.

5   With whom we have been hidden in God.

II

1   Who has become our paschal sacrifice.

2   Who shook the earth when he rose from death.

3   For whom the angel removed the stone from the tomb.

4   Who fulfilled his promise of resurrection.

5   Who, rejected, has become the cornerstone.

[Mt. 28:1–7 (Easter Vigil)]

III

1   Whose death is the seed of new life. (Guardini)

2   Who is the true Lamb that took away the sins of the world.

3   Who has made us children of light.

4   Who has opened the gates of heaven.

5   Whose perfect sacrifice fulfilled all others.

SECOND SUNDAY OF EASTER

A 1 Who gave the disciples his peace.

2 Who sent them as the Father sent him.

3 Who breathed the Holy Spirit on them.

4 Who gave them the power to forgive sins.

5 Who said to Thomas: "Believe!"

[Jn. 20:19–31]

B 1 Who called us to his kingdom.

2 In whose glory we rejoice.

3 Who gave us a new birth in the Spirit.

4 Whose love is everlasting.

5 Who—rejected—became the living cornerstone.

C 1 Who carried his apostle John up in ecstasy in Patmos.

2 Who gave him a vision of Christ.

3 Who told him to fear nothing.

4 Who told him to write down what he would see.

5 Who is the First and the Last and the Living One.

[Rev. 1:9–13; 17–19]

THIRD SUNDAY OF EASTER

A 1 Who joined two disciples on the road to Emmaus.

2 Who explained the Scriptures to them.

3 Whose words burned in their hearts.

4 Whom they urged to stay with them.

5 Whom they recognized by the breaking of the bread.

[Lk. 24:13–35]

B 1 Who stood in their midst: "Peace be with you!"

2 Who freed them from their fright.

3 Who showed them his hands and his feet.

4 Who ate from the fish they had grilled.

5 Who explained the Scriptures to them.

[Lk. 24:35–48]

C 1 Who met them at Lake Tiberias.

2 Who led them to a rich haul of fish.

3 Whom John first recognized as the Lord.

4 Who invited them to the meal he had prepared.

5 Who asked Simon Peter three times: "Do you love me more than the others?"

[Jn. 21:1–19]

FOURTH SUNDAY OF EASTER

A 1 Who said: "I am the Good Shepherd."

2 Whose voice his sheep do hear.

3 Who calls his own by name.

4 Who goes ahead of them and they follow him.

5 Who came to bring fullness of life.

[Jn. 10:1–10]

B 1 Who is the Good Shepherd.

2 Who knows his sheep and they know him.

3 Who laid down his life for his sheep.

4 Who came that we have life to the full.

5 Who wills that there be one shepherd and one flock.

[Jn. 10:11–18]

C 1 Whose sheep hear his voice and follow him.

2 Who gives them life eternal.

3 Who will not let them perish.

4 From whose arms they will not be snatched.

5 Who laid down his life for his sheep.

[Jn. 10:27–30]

FIFTH SUNDAY OF EASTER

A   1   Who called forth a new creation.

     2   Who answered man's longing for his revelation.

     3   Who is the Way, the Truth, and the Life.

     4   Whose Father is always in him, as he is in the Father.

     5   Whose works are those of the Father and the Spirit.

[Jn. 14:1–12]

B   1   Whose Eucharist reveals God's call for unity in him.

     2   Who wants us to remain in him as he in us.

     3   Who is the true vine and the Father the vinedresser.

     4   In whom we must live to bring fruit.

     5   Without whom we can do nothing.

[Jn. 15:1–8]

C   1   Whose glorification is that of the Father.

     2   Who gave us a new commandment: "Love one another."

     3   Whose love shall be extended to all the faithful.

     4   Who makes love the test of discipleship.

     5   Who called them his little children.

[Jn. 13:31–35]

SIXTH SUNDAY OF EASTER

A 1 Who has set his people free.

2 Who promised them another advocate, the Spirit of truth.

3 Whose Spirit will remain forever in our hearts.

4 Who will let us know the Divine Indwelling.

5 Who reveals himself to those who love him.

[Jn. 14:15–21]

B 1 Who loves us as the Father loves him.

2 In whose love we live, if we keep the commandments.

3 Who wants to share his joy with us.

4 Whose love has chosen us to go and bear fruit.

5 Who calls us his friends.

[Jn. 15:9–17]

C 1 Whom to love means to keep his commandments.

2 Who promised them the Advocate.

3 Whose Spirit will teach them everything.

4 Whose Spirit will dwell in them forever.

5 Who left them his peace which the world cannot give.

[Jn. 14:23–29]

ASCENSION

A 1 Who is with us always until the end of the world.

2 Who prepared them to teach the Good News to all nations.

3 Who made them his witnesses in Jerusalem.

4 Who was lifted before their eyes to heaven.

5 Who took his seat at the right hand of God.

[Acts 1:1–11]

B 1 Who sent them to proclaim the Good News to the whole world.

2 Who gave them the power of healing.

3 Who was taken up to heaven.

4 Who took his seat at the right hand of the Father.

5 Who confirmed them by his signs.

[Mk. 16:15–20]

C 1 Who interpreted the Scriptures to them.

2 Who asked them to preach penance for the forgiving of sins.

3 Who sent them out as witnesses.

4 Who blessed them and was carried up to heaven.

5 Whose apostles proclaimed the praises of God.

[Lk. 24:46–53]

SEVENTH SUNDAY OF EASTER

A 1 Who prayed that the Father glorify him.

2 Who gives eternal life to those entrusted to him.

3 Who finished the work the Father had given him.

4 Whose teaching and work is that of the Father.

5 Who is glorified in his apostles.

[Jn. 17:1–11]

B 1 Who prayed for their unity, that they be one.

2 Who prayed for the Divine protection of the Church.

3 Who prayed that they be protected from the evil one.

4 Who consecrated himself for their sakes.

5 Who asked the Father to consecrate them in the truth.

[Jn. 17:11–19]

C 1 Who prayed for the unity of all who believe in him.

2 Who prayed for the unity of the Church.

3 Who prayed that the Church fulfill its mission.

4 Whose Divine presence remains with the Church.

5 Who continues his work through the Holy Spirit.

[Jn. 17:20–26]

PENTECOST VIGIL

1 Whose Spirit has poured his love into our hearts.

2 Whose Spirit gives us new life.

3 Who said: "If anyone thirsts let him come to me!"

4 Who gives living water that creates rivers of eternal life.

5 Who kindles in us the fire of his Divine love.

PENTECOST SUNDAY

I

1 Whose Spirit fills the whole world.

2 Whose Spirit poured out God's love into our hearts.

3 Whose Spirit appeared over them in fiery tongues.

4 Whose Spirit made them talk in foreign languages.

5 Whose Spirit prompted them to make bold
   proclamations.

II

1 Who is the Father of the poor.

2 Who is the giver of God's gifts.

3 Who brings relief and consolation.

4 Who brings relief to those weary with toil.

5 Who comforts the sorrowful.

III

1 Without whose aid man can do nothing.

2 Who washes clean the sinful soul.

3 Who cherishes and warms the ice-cold heart.

4 Who gives direction to the wayward.

5 Whose seven holy gifts bring us salvation.

[Sequence of Pentecost]

SEASON OF THE YEAR

SECOND SUNDAY OF THE YEAR

A 1 In whom we are consecrated to God.

2 Who is the Lamb that takes away
the sins of the world.

3 Who is above John and was before him.

4 Upon whom John saw the Spirit descend.

5 Who is God's Chosen one.

[Jn. 1:29–34]

B 1 Who made us temples of the Holy Spirit.

2 Who has purchased us at a high price.

3 Who came to do the Father's will.

4 About whom John witnessed: "There is the Lamb of
God."

5 Whom two of John's disciples followed.

C 1 Whose mother told him at Cana that they had no wine.

2 Who replied that his hour had not yet come.

3 Whose mother told the servants: "Do whatever he tells
you."

4 Who changed the water into wine at God's time.

5 Who revealed his glory and whose disciples believed in
him.

[Jn. 2:1–12]

THIRD SUNDAY OF THE YEAR

A 1 Who lives in holiness and glory.

2 Whose light has shone upon the land of darkness.

3 Who has brought abundant joy and great rejoicing.

4 Who proclaimed the Kingdom of Heaven.

5 Who told them to reform their lives.

B 1 Who proclaimed the Good News from God.

2 Whose kingdom is close at hand.

3 Who said that we should repent.

4 Who warns us to reform our lives.

5 Who chose followers to become fishers of men.

[Mk. 1:14–20]

C 1 Who read in the synagogue of Nazareth.

2 To whom the Spirit of the Lord was given.

3 Who read: "He has anointed me."

4 "Who has sent me to bring glad tidings to the poor."

5 Who said: "This text is fulfilled today."

[Lk. 1:1–4; 4:14–21]

FOURTH SUNDAY OF THE YEAR

A 1 Who promised the Kingdom of Heaven to the poor.

2 Who brings comfort to the mourners.

3 Who shows mercy to the merciful.

4 Who reveals his face to the pure in heart.

5 Who calls peacemakers the sons of God.

[Mt. 5:1–12]

B 1 Who wants us to be free of all worries.

2 Who wants us to pursue holiness in body and spirit.

3 Who drove an unclean spirit out of a man.

4 About whom they were amazed.

5 Who brought a new teaching, with authority behind it.

C 1 Who said: "This text is fulfilled today."

2 To whom they replied: "Is that not Joseph's Son?"

3 Who said: "No prophet is accepted in his own country."

4 About whom enraged, they tried to throw down the cliff.

5 Who slipped through the crowd and walked away.

[Lk. 4:21–30]

FIFTH SUNDAY OF THE YEAR

A 1 Who tells us to be merciful.

2 Who calls a just man "a light in the darkness."

3 Who said: "You are the salt of the earth."

4 Who said: "You are the light of the world."

5 Who said: "Let men see your good works."

B 1 Who healed Simon's mother-in-law.

2 Who healed people of various afflictions.

3 Who cast out many devils.

4 Who went into the desert to pray to his Father.

5 Who proclaimed the Good News in neighboring towns.

[Mk. 1:29–39]

C 1 Who taught the crowds from the boat.

2 Who told them to put out into deep water.

3 Upon whose word the nets filled to the breaking.

4 Whom Peter asked to leave: "I am a sinful man."

5 Who made Peter the fisher of men.

[Lk. 5:1–11]

SIXTH SUNDAY OF THE YEAR

A 1 Who taught a new way of life: perfect love.

2 Who asks us to forgive a brother's anger.

3 Who condemned impurity, even in thought.

4 Who requires truthfulness—in reverence to Truth.

5 Who demands self-denial to obtain eternal life.

[Mt. 5:17–37]

B 1 Who was asked by a leper to cure him.

2 Who had compassion and healed him.

3 Who sent him to the priests to fulfill the law.

4 Who said: "Not a word to anyone, now."

5 Whose reputation grew so he could not enter towns openly.

[Mk. 1:40–45]

C 1 Whose kingdom belongs to the poor.

2 Who will satisfy the hungry.

3 Who will make joyful those who mourn.

4 Who will reward in heaven those persecuted on earth.

5 Who has compassion with our suffering.

[Lk. 6:17, 20–26]

SEVENTH SUNDAY OF THE YEAR

A   1   Who said to love all men.

     2   Who said to love even our enemies.

     3   Who taught that love will overcome hatred.

     4   Who is the image of forgiving.

     5   Who said: "Be perfect as your heavenly Father is."

[Mt. 5:38–48]

B   1   To whom they brought a paralytic for healing.

     2   Who said to him: "Your sins are forgiven."

     3   Who sensed the scandalous thoughts of the scribes.

     4   Who healed the sick man.

     5   Who thus proved his Divinity.

[Mk. 2:1–12]

C   1   Who taught to love our enemies.

     2   Who said to do good to those who hate us.

     3   Who taught to be compassionate as our Father is compassionate.

     4   Through whom we overcome evil by blessing.

     5   Who taught generosity in giving through faith.

[Lk. 6:27–38]

EIGHTH SUNDAY OF THE YEAR

A 1 Who said: "No man can serve two masters."

2 Who said not to worry anxiously over earthly needs.

3 Whose Father knows our needs and will provide.

4 Who said to seek the Kingdom of Heaven first.

5 Who said that all other things will be added.

[Mt. 6:24–33]

B 1 Whom the Pharisees questioned about the non-fasting of the apostles.

2 Who answered that fasting is inopportune at a wedding.

3 Who predicted the apostles' fasting after the groom is taken away.

4 Who told them: "New wine, fresh skins."

5 Who prepared his apostles for a new *way* of life.

[Mk. 2:18–22]

C 1 Who warned: no blind man can guide another.

2 Who said to begin correction with self.

3 Who taught that renewal comes from good example.

4 Who taught that only the good can do good.

5 Who makes us holy in truth.

[Lk. 6:39–45]

NINTH SUNDAY OF THE YEAR

A 1 Who challenges us to build our life on solid faith.

2 Who said hearing the word is not enough.

3 Whose heaven enter those who do the will of God.

4 Who calls the doer of God's will a sensible builder.

5 Who taught with authority—in a new spirit.

[Mt. 7:21–27]

B 1 Who revealed God's glory on his face.

2 Who wants us to reveal God's glory to men.

3 Who went on in spite of all difficulties.

4 In whom we are dying continually.

5 For whom we are delivered to death constantly.

[2 Cor. 4:6–11]

C 1 Who was asked by a centurion to heal his servant.

2 Who offered to go to his house.

3 To whom the centurion confessed his unworthiness.

4 In whose healing power the centurion had deep faith.

5 Who marveled at his faith and healed his servant.

[Lk. 7:1–10]

TENTH SUNDAY OF THE YEAR

A 1 Who gives us new life through the Spirit.

   2 Who shows his saving power to the upright.

   3 Who has words of everlasting life.

   4 Who came to call sinners.

   5 Who came to heal the sick.

B 1 Whose Spirit teaches his truth.

   2 With whom is mercy and fullness of redemption.

   3 In whom my soul trusts.

   4 Who provides a home for us in heaven.

   5 Whose family are those who do the will of God.

C 1 Who met the funeral procession at Naim.

   2 Who had compassion with the mother's sorrow.

   3 Who raised the youth back to life.

   4 Who gave him back to his mother.

   5 In whom God has visited his people.

[Lk. 7:11–17]

ELEVENTH SUNDAY OF THE YEAR

A 1 Who had compassion with the crowds.

2 Who felt they were like sheep without a shepherd.

3 Who gave the apostles the power to heal the sick.

4 Who sent them to the lost sheep of Israel.

5 Who sent them to proclaim the kingdom of heaven.

[Mt. 9:36–10:8]

B 1 Who sows the kingdom of God into the world.

2 Whose harvest is small at first like the mustard seed.

3 Whose harvest will develop into a large tree.

4 To whose tree the birds will come.

5 In whose tree I build my nest.

[Mk. 4:26–34]

C 1 Whose feet were washed with the tears of a sinful woman.

2 Whose feet were dried with her hair.

3 Whose feet were anointed with precious oil.

4 Who forgave her much because she loved much.

5 Who forgives little to those whose love is small.

[Lk. 7:36–8:3]

TWELFTH SUNDAY OF THE YEAR

A 1 Who told them to witness boldly and publicly.

2 Who told them to fear God alone.

3 Whose Father cares for sparrows.

4 Whose followers are worth much more than sparrows.

5 Whose reward for fidelity is eternal life.

[Mt. 10:26–33]

B 1 Who slept during a storm on the lake.

2 Whose apostles woke him for fear of drowning.

3 Who rebuked the wind and the waves.

4 Who quieted the raging elements.

5 Whose apostles were awed by him and his power.

[Mk. 4:35–41]

C 1 For whom my soul is thirsting.

2 Who made us sons of God.

3 Whose words are spirit and life.

4 To whom Peter confessed: "You are the Messiah!"

5 Whose disciple must take up his cross daily.

THIRTEENTH SUNDAY OF THE YEAR

A 1   Who claims the whole heart of man.

   2   Whose disciple must carry his cross.

   3   Who demands total surrender from the disciple.

   4   Who rewards hospitality given for his sake.

   5   Who rewards even a cup of water given for his sake.

[Mt. 10:37–42]

B 1   Whom Jairus asked to heal his daughter.

   2   Who was told that the child was dead.

   3   Who said to Jairus: "Believe and have faith!"

   4   Who was ridiculed by the bystanders.

   5   Who restored the little girl back to life.

[Mk. 5:21–43]

C 1   Whose disciple must give up family and home.

   2   Whose home is work for the Kingdom.

   3   Who requests total dedication from his disciple.

   4   Who wants his followers spiritually alive.

   5   Who demands a radical break with the past to start a new way.

[Lk. 9:51–62]

FOURTEENTH SUNDAY OF THE YEAR

A 1 Who reveals himself to the mere children.

     2 Who refreshes all the weary who come to him.

     3 Who invites us to accept his yoke: it is easy.

     4 Who invites us to learn from him.

     5 Who is gentle and humble of heart.

[Mt. 11:25–30]

B 1 Who became man and lived among us.

     2 Who makes all those who accept him children of God.

     3 Who taught the word of God in Nazareth.

     4 Who was rejected in his home town.

     5 Who suffered the fate of prophets.

[Mk. 6:1–6]

C 1 Who sent his disciples to proclaim the Good News.

     2 Who sent them as lambs among the wolves.

     3 Who forbade purse and haversack.

     4 Who asked them to pass on his peace.

     5 Who gave them the power to heal the sick.

[Lk. 10:1–12]

FIFTEENTH SUNDAY OF THE YEAR

A   1   Who sowed the seed of the Kingdom of God.

2   Whose seed on the footpath was eaten by birds.

3   Whose seed on rocky ground died for lack of roots.

4   Whose seed among thorns was choked.

5   Whose seed on good soil yielded grain hundredfold.

[Mt. 13:1–9]

B   1   Who blessed us with all spiritual blessings.

2   Who chose us before the world was made.

3   Through whom the Father adopted us as his sons.

4   Through whose blood we have been redeemed.

5   Whose wisdom taught us the mystery of redemption.

[Eph. 1:3–14]

C   1   Who is the image of the invisible God.

2   Through whom we know the Father.

3   In whom, through whom, and for whom everything was created.

4   Who *is* before all else that is.

5   Who is the head of the Mystical Body.

[Col. 1:15–20]

SIXTEENTH SUNDAY OF THE YEAR

A 1 Who sowed good seed in his field.

   2 Whose enemy sowed weeds through the wheat.

   3 Whose servants asked whether to pull the weeds.

   4 Who will wait until harvest time.

   5 Who will burn the weeds and collect the wheat
       into his barn.

[Mt. 13:24–30]

B 1 Who was tender with his apostles.

   2 Who invited them to "rest awhile."

   3 Who was followed by a vast crowd.

   4 Who had pity "because they were like lost sheep."

   5 Who fed their spiritual hunger.

[Mk. 6:30–34]

C 1 Who praised Mary who "had chosen the better part."

   2 Who warns the Marthas who are too anxious.

   3 Who wants us to base everything on the inner life.

   4 Who often retired to pray to his Father.

   5 Who went up the mountain to be with God.

[Lk. 10:38–42]

SEVENTEENTH SUNDAY OF THE YEAR

A   1   Who compared God's Kingdom to a treasure buried in a field.

2   For whose Kingdom some sacrifice all they possess.

3   Who compared God's Kingdom to a valuable pearl.

4   For whose pearl some give all they own.

5   Who gives the ALL for the all.

[Mt. 13:44–46]

B   1   Who gives us food in due season.

2   Who had compassion with the hungry crowd.

3   Under whose blessing the bread multiplied miraculously.

4   Whom they wanted to proclaim a Jewish Messiah.

5   Who escaped to the hill by himself.

[Jn. 6:1–15]

C   1   Who taught them how to pray.

2   Who said: "Ask, and you shall be given."

3   Who said: "Search, and you will find."

4   Who said: "Knock, and the door will be opened."

5   Whose Father gives the Holy Spirit to those who ask.

[Lk. 11:1–13]

EIGHTEENTH SUNDAY OF THE YEAR

A 1 Who had compassion and healed their sick.

2 Who had pity with the hungry crowd.

3 Who looked up to heaven and said the blessing.

4 Who broke the bread and fed five thousand.

5 Who is the bread of life.

[Mt. 14:13–21]

B 1 Who told them to have faith in God's messenger.

2 Whom they asked for a sign, such as manna from heaven.

3 Whose Father gives the bread from heaven.

4 Whom they asked for this bread.

5 Who stated: "I am the bread of life."

[Jn. 6:24–35]

C 1 Who said to seek the things that are above.

2 Who reminds us that our treasure is in heaven.

3 Who said to seek the Kingdom first.

4 Who said to lay up treasures in heaven.

5 Who knows our heart will be with our treasure.

[Lk. 12:13–21]

NINETEENTH SUNDAY OF THE YEAR

A 1   Who walked on the storm-tossed sea.

2   Whom the apostles mistook for a ghost.

3   Who said: "It is I. Do not be afraid."

4   Who saved Peter, whose faith had wavered.

5   To whom they showed reverence as their Messiah.

[Mt. 14:22–33]

B 1   To whom nobody comes unless the Father draws him.

2   Who alone knows the Father.

3   Who raises us up on the last day.

4   Who is the living bread come down from heaven.

5   Who gives eternal life.

[Jn. 6:41–51]

C 1   Who told them to lay up spiritual wealth.

2   Who told them to be awake and active.

3   Who will wait on those who are prepared.

4   Who said: "You must stand ready."

5   Who will come unexpectedly.

[Lk. 12:35–40]

TWENTIETH SUNDAY OF THE YEAR

A 1 Whom a Canaanite woman asked to heal her daughter.

2 Whose mission was only "to the lost sheep of Israel."

3 Who did not want "to throw the children's bread to the dogs."

4 To whom she said: "Even the dogs eat the scraps from their master's table."

5 Who rewarded her faith by healing her daughter.

[Mt. 15:21–28]

B 1 Who is the living bread from heaven.

2 Who is the food of our life.

3 Through whom I live, as he through the Father.

4 In whom I am, and he in me.

5 Through whom I live forever.

[Jn. 6:51–58]

C 1 Who came to bring fire to the earth.

2 Whose fire is the ardor of a new creation.

3 Whose love was anxious for the baptism of death.

4 Whose battle was against worldliness.

5 Who confronted it with the glory of the Kingdom.

[Lk. 12:49–53]

TWENTY-FIRST SUNDAY OF THE YEAR

A   1   Whose wisdom and knowledge are deep.

     2   Whose motives are beyond our understanding.

     3   Whose mind nobody has known.

     4   Who is the way, the truth, and the life.

     5   Through whom alone we come to the Father.

B   1   Whose flesh and blood give eternal life.

     2   Whose words are spirit, and they are life.

     3   To whom we come only by the grace of the Father.

     4   Whom Peter confessed as God's Holy One.

     5   Who called them his friends.

[Jn. 6:60–69]

C   1   Whose salvation is for all mankind.

     2   Who will set a sign among them.

     3   Whom all nations will worship in Jerusalem.

     4   Whose glory all nations shall proclaim.

     5   Who warned them to "come in through the narrow door."

TWENTY-SECOND SUNDAY OF THE YEAR

A 1 Who predicted his passion, death, and resurrection.

2 Whose Cross is the beacon for every Christian.

3 Whose follower must deny himself to make room for Christ.

4 Whose Cross we must accept to find our soul.

5 Who gives life to those who lose it for his sake.

[Mt. 16:21–27]

B 1 Who denounced the lip service and formalism of the Pharisees.

2 Who saw through the emptiness of their religious practices.

3 Who recognized their insincerity and hypocrisy.

4 Who declared purity a matter of the heart.

5 Who taught to obey God rather than men.

[Mk. 7:1–8; 14–15; 21–23]

C 1 Who noticed how some picked the places of honor.

2 Who said: "Take the lowest place."

3 Who said: "Let the host move you higher."

4 Who humbled himself to the death on the Cross.

5 Whose Father raised him to the summit of heaven.

[Lk. 14:1; 7–14]

TWENTY-THIRD SUNDAY OF THE YEAR

A 1 Who taught to forgive a brother who hurt us.

2 Who said that we must overcome our natural reaction of hatred.

3 Who taught to free ourselves from all resentment.

4 Whose way opens our hearts to God's grace.

5 Who links our forgiveness with that of the Father.

[Mt. 18:15–20]

B 1 To whom they brought a man who could neither hear nor talk.

2 Who led him away from the crowd.

3 Who touched his ears and his tongue.

4 Who said: "Be thou opened."

5 Who healed his deafness and speech defect.

[Mk. 7:31–37]

C 1 Who demands total dedication from his disciples.

2 Whose followers must give up family ties and even self.

3 Whose follower must carry his cross.

4 Who recommends careful consideration before making this decision.

5 Whose follower must renounce all his possessions.

[Lk. 14:25–33]

TWENTY-FOURTH SUNDAY OF THE YEAR

A 1 Who said to forgive seventy times seven times.

2 Who knows it can be done only with the grace of God.

3 Whose Father forgives huge debts to sinners.

4 Whose Father condemns those who do not do likewise.

5 Who warns us to forgive from our whole heart.

[Mt. 18:21–35]

B 1 Whom Peter acknowledged openly as the Messiah.

2 Who tried to teach them the idea of a suffering Messiah.

3 Who rebuked Peter's zealous remonstration.

4 Who obeyed his Father's plan of Messiahship.

5 Who makes carrying the cross the sign of discipleship.

[Mk. 8:27–35]

C 1 Who came to call sinners.

2 Who goes after the lost sheep until he finds it.

3 Who rejoices over finding the lost sheep.

4 Whose angels rejoice over one repentant sinner.

5 Whose Father rejoiced because his son, dead, had come back to life.

[Lk. 15:1–32]

TWENTY-FIFTH SUNDAY OF THE YEAR

A 1 Who went out to hire workmen for his vineyard.

2 Who hired them all hours of the day.

3 Who gave them each a day's wages.

4 Who is free to be generous.

5 Who makes the last to be first.

[Mt. 20:1–16]

B 1 Who predicted his suffering, death, and resurrection.

2 Who said the first must be last and the servant of all.

3 Who set a little child in front of them.

4 Who said: "Whoever welcomes a child in my name welcomes me."

5 Who said: "He who welcomes me welcomes him who sent me."

[Mk. 9:30–37]

C 1 Who praised the shrewdness of the dishonest steward.

2 Who warns against the dangers of wealth.

3 Who recommends to use it wisely, in terms of eternity.

4 Who said that no servant can belong to two masters.

5 Who said: "You cannot serve God and mammon."

[Lk. 16:1–13]

TWENTY-SIXTH SUNDAY OF THE YEAR

A 1 Who declared action the test of obedience.

2 Who contrasted the leaders' pride with the sinners' humility.

3 Who forgives the penitent sinner.

4 Who saw the penitent sinner advance into the Kingdom.

5 Whose forerunner John had shown the way of righteousness.

[Mt. 21:28–32]

B 1 Who taught tolerance toward others who work in his name.

2 Who rewards the smallest service given for his sake.

3 Who will severely punish those who scandalize simple believers.

4 Whose followers must sacrifice everything to avoid scandal.

5 Who said to save nothing to gain eternal life.

[Mk. 9:38–43, 45, 47–48]

C 1 Who told them about the rich man and poor Lazarus.

2 Who warns against the inordinate use of wealth.

3 Who said that the poor on earth may be rich in eternity.

4 Who knew the poor are more open to God's teaching.

5 Whose Father's law is all we need.

[Lk. 16:19–31]

TWENTY-SEVENTH SUNDAY OF
THE YEAR

A   1   Whose Father is the owner of the vineyard.

2   Whose messengers were abused and killed.

3   Whose only Son was killed.

4   Who, rejected by the builders, became the cornerstone.

5   Who predicted the Kingdom would pass to those who will produce fruit.

[Mt. 21:33–43]

B   1   Who taught that divorce is contrary to God's law.

2   Who had tender love for children.

3   Who said: "Let the children come to me."

4   Who said that the Kingdom of God belonged to them.

5   Who embraced and blessed the children.

[Mk. 10:2–16]

C   1   Whom the apostles asked for an increase in faith.

2   Who wanted their faith alive like a mustard seed.

3   Who admonished them to keep toiling.

4   Who wants us to remain humble.

5   Whose Spirit alone does all the good in us.

[Lk. 17:5–10]

TWENTY-EIGHTH SUNDAY OF THE YEAR

A 1 Who will prepare for all peoples on Mount Zion.

2 Who will remove all barriers between nations.

3 Who will destroy Death forever.

4 Who will wipe away the tears from every cheek.

5 Whose hand will rest on Mount Zion.

[Is. 25:6–10]

B 1 Whose word discerns the most inward intentions of our heart.

2 Who calls some to a higher life.

3 Who demands renouncing all earthly wealth for perfection.

4 Whose requirements scared his disciples.

5 Through whom all things are possible with God.

[Mk. 10:17–27]

C 1 Whom ten lepers asked for healing.

2 Who had pity and healed them fully.

3 To whom only a Samaritan showed gratitude.

4 Who praised him for his faith.

5 Who reveals his Kingdom to little ones.

[Lk. 17:11–19]

TWENTY-NINTH SUNDAY OF THE YEAR

A 1 Whom the Pharisees tried to trap.

2 Whom they asked about paying taxes to Rome.

3 Who recognized the dilemma of their question.

4 Who said: "Give to Caesar what belongs to Caesar."

5 Who said: "Give to God what belongs to God."

[Mt. 22:15–21]

B 1 Through whose suffering many are justified.

2 In whom we have the supreme high priest.

3 Who was tempted as we—but is without sin.

4 Who gives us mercy and help in time of need.

5 Who gave his life in ransom for many.

C 1 Who said: "Pray continually."

2 Who said not to lose heart.

3 Who said to importune until prayer is granted.

4 Who will grant the prayers of the just man.

5 Who wondered whether he will find faith at his last coming.

[Lk. 18:1–8]

THIRTIETH SUNDAY OF THE YEAR

A 1 Who made love of God the greatest commandment.

2 Who said to love God with our whole being.

3 Who said: "The second commandment is like it."

4 Who said: "Love your neighbor as yourself."

5 Who made love of God and neighbor the law of life.

[Mt. 22:34–40]

B 1 Whom a blind beggar asked for pity.

2 Who asked: "What do you want me to do?"

3 Whom the blind man asked for his sight.

4 Who rewarded his faith and made him see.

5 Who is the light of the world.

[Mk. 10:46–52]

C 1 To whom all my sins are known.

2 Who saw the self-righteousness of the Pharisee.

3 Who saw the humility of the penitent tax collector.

4 Who said that the tax collector went home justified.

5 Who will exalt the humble.

[Lk. 18:9–14]

THIRTY-FIRST SUNDAY OF THE YEAR

A 1 Who told them to observe the laws of the Pharisees.

2 Who warned them not to follow their actions.

3 Who warned against the Pharisees' vanity for first places.

4 Who said the greatest among them must be their servant.

5 Who will exalt him who humbles himself.

[Mt. 23:1–12]

B 1 Who made love of God the first commandment.

2 Who said to love God with all our strength.

3 Who said to love our neighbor as ourselves.

4 Who taught that they are the greatest commandments.

5 Who said that they are linked together.

[Mk. 12:28–34]

C 1 Who was a friend to Zacchaeus, the tax collector.

2 Who chose his house to stay at.

3 Who brought salvation to his whole house.

4 Who brought redemption to the sons of Abraham.

5 Who came to seek and save what was lost.

[Lk. 19:1–10]

THIRTY-SECOND SUNDAY OF THE YEAR

A 1 Who told the parable of the bridesmaids.

2 Who warns us to be ready and stay awake.

3 Who tests our faith in waiting.

4 Who provides our strength in hoping.

5 Whose love provides the oil of our sanctification.

[Mt. 25:1–13]

B 1 Who did not enter a sanctuary made by man.

2 Who entered heaven and appeared before God for us.

3 Who offered up once and for all.

4 Who did away with sin by sacrificing himself.

5 Who will appear again to bring salvation.

[Heb. 9:24–28]

C 1 Who said: "The children of this world marry."

2 Who calls the children of God to the pursuit of virginity.

3 Who frees their souls from worldly cares.

4 Who said that they live for God.

5 Who is the God of the living.

[Lk. 20:27, 34–38]

THIRTY-THIRD SUNDAY OF THE YEAR

A 1 Who gives us talents to build up his Kingdom.

2 Who asks us to use them and toil constantly.

3 Whose true servant is prudent and faithful.

4 Who will provide the joy of heaven to the faithful servant.

5 Who will thrust the lazy servant into the dark.

[Mt. 25:14–30]

B 1 Whose signs will appear in the heaven.

2 Who will come at the appointed time.

3 Who will appear with great power and glory.

4 Whose angels will gather his chosen ones.

5 Who warns us to be prepared at all times.

[Mk. 13:24–32]

C 1 Who predicted the destruction of Jerusalem.

2 Who foretold the persecution of the apostles.

3 Who said they would become witnesses for him.

4 Who promised to protect them by his word and wisdom.

5 Who said: "Your endurance will win your lives."

[Lk. 21:5–19]

THIRTY-FOURTH OR LAST SUNDAY OF THE YEAR—CHRIST THE KING

A 1 Who is the Lamb that was slain.

2 Who is worthy to receive strength and godhead.

3 Who is worthy of wisdom and power and honor.

4 To whom be power and glory forever.

5 Who is the King of Kings, the Lord of Lords.

[Rev. 5:12; 1:6]

B 1 Who is Christ, the King of the universe.

2 Whose glory pervades heaven and earth.

3 Who was crucified with criminals.

4 Who "has done nothing wrong!"

5 Whose Cross is the scepter of his glory.

C 1 Who rescued us from the power of darkness.

2 Who is the image of the invisible God.

3 Who is the first-born of all creation.

4 Who made peace by his death on the Cross.

5 Whom the Father set as King over the whole creation.

[Col. 1:12–20]

SOLEMNITIES OF THE LORD DURING THE SEASON OF THE YEAR

SUNDAY AFTER PENTECOST—
TRINITY SUNDAY

A 1 Whose coming revealed to us the Trinity.

   2 Whose Father's wisdom created the universe.

   3 Whose humanity redeemed mankind.

   4 Who sanctifies us through the Holy Spirit.

   5 Whose Holy Spirit is the Love between Father and Son.

B 1 Who disclosed to us the hidden life of God.

   2 Who revealed to us the goodness of the Father.

   3 Who brought us the truth and redemption of love.

   4 Who sent us the fire of the Holy Spirit.

   5 Whose eternal life must become our dwelling.

C 1 Whose Father adopted us as his children.

   2 Whose humanity made us brothers and sisters.

   3 Whose Spirit unites us to God through love.

   4 Whose life in us develops faith, hope, and charity.

   5 Whose grace in us is the image of the Trinity.

THURSDAY AFTER TRINITY SUNDAY— CORPUS CHRISTI

A 1 Who fed his people with the finest wheat.

     2 Who is the living bread come down from heaven.

     3 Whose body makes us live forever.

     4 Through whom I live as he through the Father.

     5 Who lives in me and I in him.

[Jn. 6:51–58]

B 1 Who took bread, blessed and broke it.

     2 Who gave it to his disciples: "This is my body."

     3 Who gave thanks and passed the cup to them.

     4 Who said: "This is my blood, the blood of the new covenant."

     5 Whose oblation is the sacrifice of our peace with God.

[Mk. 14:12–16]

C 1 Who is the living bread come down from heaven.

     2 Whose feeding of the five thousand anticipated the Eucharist.

     3 Who is the high priest forever according to Melchisedech.

     4 Whose Eucharist is the memorial of his Passion.

     5 Whose Eucharist is the eternal call of God's love.

[Lk. 9:11–17]

FRIDAY AFTER THE SECOND SUNDAY AFTER PENTECOST—SACRED HEART

A 1 Who revealed God's mysteries to the little ones.

2 Who is gentle and humble of heart.

3 Who invites us to learn from him.

4 Who gives rest to the burdened.

5 Who invites us to accept his yoke.

[Mt. 11:25–30]

B 1 Whose love is greater than all knowledge.

2 Who revealed God's infinite wisdom to us.

3 Who wants to live in our hearts.

4 Whose side was pierced by a lance.

5 From whose heart flow streams of living water.

C 1 Who watches over his flock as a shepherd.

2 Who rescues them from mist and darkness.

3 Who feeds them on good grazing ground.

4 Who looks for the stray and bandages the wounded.

5 Who is the Divine shepherd.

[Ez. 34:11–16]

APPENDIX

MEDITATION SUGGESTIONS ON VARIOUS ASPECTS OF SPIRITUAL LIFE

HOW TO USE THE APPENDIX

With regard to the use of the appendix: It is used differently than the liturgical part of the book. It offers meditations for various life situations and spiritual needs. How they are used depends on the individual. Our prayers vary, our needs of relating to God vary. The best I can say: The meditations are offered for the selection of the worshiper. He may select from them as he does from his pantry and refrigerator: select the spiritual food that seems indicated at the moment. The table of contents on page 9 gives the headings of meditation suggestions according to content: The heading is a guide to the nature of the meditation.

Meditations from the psalms have been included because of their strength-providing elements; the selections from the Church Fathers because of their closeness to God; the excerpts from spiritual writers because of their pregnant illumination of matters of faith, or significant contributions to spirituality. Every worshiper can select that which might seem most helpful to him. Those among the worshipers who do not find the time to do much spiritual reading may find that some excerpts are better than nothing. Others, who are able to spend time in spiritual reading, might be induced by the material offered here to seek the sources themselves.

GOD IN MY HEART

1 Who is present and dwells within me.

[Raoul]

2 Who made us temples of the Holy Spirit.

[St. Paul]

3 Whom we find in the cell of our heart.

[St. Catherine of Siena]

4 Who is the gardener of our soul.

[St. Teresa of Ávila]

5 Whom we find if we seek him.

[St. Augustine]

CHRIST, OUR WAY TO THE FATHER

1 Who is the Way which leads to the Father.

2 Who is the Light that destroys the darkness.

3 Who is the Truth that does not lead us astray.

4 Who is the Bread that nourishes us to eternal life.

5 Who is the Strength that upholds us in our weakness.

OUR TREASURE

1   Whom we should seek within our heart.
                                    [Neophas the Solitary]

2   Whose treasure eye hath not seen.
                                    [1 Cor. 2:9]

3   Who gives clear vision to those sober in heart.
                                    [A Church Father]

4   Whose flame purifies the lover.
                                    [Father Antony]

5   Who said: "Where your treasure is, there your heart will be."
                                    [Mt. 6:21]

JOHANNES CHRYSOSTOM'S GOLDEN CHAIN OF BEATITUDES

1   Blessed are the humble, who also mourn for their sins.

2   Blessed are the mourners who also are meek and merciful.

3   Blessed are the merciful who are also pure of heart.

4   Blessed are the pure of heart who are peacemakers.

5   Blessed are all those who have attained to all the virtues.

[Saint John Chrysostom's interpretation of the Sermon on the Mount from *The Preaching of Chrysostom,* edited by Jaroslav Pelikan, Philadelphia, Fortress Press, 1967, p. 52. Copyright © 1967 and reprinted with the permission of the publisher.]

THE WHEAT OF CHRIST

1   Who said that the grain of wheat must die before it can produce fruit.

2   Whose martyr Bishop Ignatius longed to follow Christ in his Passion.

3   Whose martyr Ignatius desired to be ground up by wild animals to end up as pure bread of Christ.

4   Who is manifest the more that he is hidden in God.

5   In whose Cross we glory with St. Ignatius.

REFORMATION IN CHRIST

1   Who calls us to ceaseless spiritual labor.

2   Whose saints struggled heroically.

3   Who calls us to self-denial and mortification.

[1 Cor. 9:24–27]

4   Who calls each one at a different time.

[Mt. 20:1–16]

5   Who provides the weapons for our spiritual combat.

ETERNAL ADVENT

I

1 Whose coming was proclaimed by the prophets.

2 For whose coming all mankind had been waiting.

3 For whose love our hearts are yearning.

4 Whose advent is an eternal coming into our souls.

5 Whose coming is the pledge of our redemption.

II

1 Whom we find in abiding in him.

2 Who is always near and will come soon.

3 Who comes nearer as faith does grow.

4 Who is close to us in all the sacraments.

5 Whose Eucharist is the home of our soul.

THE COMBAT OF LIFE

1 Who anoints us with his grace to strengthen us for the battle.

2 Who helps me after a fall and sets me on my feet again.

3 Who has put on us an armor stronger than steel.

4 Who has given me the shield of faith.

5 Who has given me the sword of the Spirit.

[John Chrysostom]

GOD IS MY ALL

1 Apart from whom I have no happiness.

2 With whom at my right hand nothing can shake me.

3 In whom my heart exults and my soul rejoices.

4 Who will not abandon my soul to Sheol.

5 Who will show me the path that leads to life.

[Ps. 16]

SIN AND REDEMPTION

I

1   Who loved the prodigal who repented.

2   Who forgave much to Mary Magdalene because she loved much.

3   Who forgave the penitent thief.

4   Who carried our sins up on the Cross.

5   Who came to "seek what was lost."

II

1   Who gave his life for our sins.

2   Who set us free from this evil age.

[Gal. 1:4]

3   Whose face has renewed the earth.

4   Whose holiness teaches us the fear of God.

5   In whom we are created anew.

PATIENCE IN SUFFERING

I

1   Who gave us an example to bear all suffering.

2   Who submitted to his Father's will in suffering.

3   Whose will must become our will in suffering.

4   Who invited us to follow him on the way of the Cross.

5   Whose trial I must not waste but use toward the redemption of the world.

II

1   Whose Cross is the gift he gives his friends.

[St. Teresa of Ávila]

2   Whose Cross is the tree of life.

3   Whose Cross is the ladder to heaven.

4   Whose Cross is the anchor that steadies our boats.

5   Whose Cross is the beacon in the storms of life.

GOD WITHIN US

1   To whom we draw near when we enter our nothingness.

2   Whom we must seek in ourselves.

3   Who requires a soul empty and free from care, depending on him alone.

4   Whom we must beg with fervent and humble sighs for Divine help.

5   From whose holy mountain we should not descend.

> [*The Plain Path to Christian Perfection*
> Johannes Tauler, 1290–1361]

SPIRITUAL RENEWAL

1   Who summons us to renew our inner self.

2   Who wants to live in our hearts.

3   Whose love is beyond all knowledge and imagination.

4   Whose power strengthens us in all dangers.

5   To whom we should pray unceasingly.

> [Eph. 4:24; 3:17, 19; 6:10, 18]

CHRIST'S HUMILITY AND GREATNESS

I

1 Whose state was divine.

2 Who did not cling to his equality with God.

3 Who emptied himself and assumed the condition of a slave.

4 Who became man and humbled himself.

5 Who became obedient unto death, even death on the Cross.

II

1 Whose Father gave him the name that is greater than any other name.

2 In honor of whose name all beings should bend their knees, in heaven and on earth.

3 Whom every tongue should acclaim Jesus Christ as Lord.

4 Who is the Lord to the glory of the Father.

5 Who gave us an example of humility and obedience.

[Phil. 2:5–11]

MAN'S RELATIONSHIP WITH GOD

1   Who is the Truth on which all earthly truths are based.

2   Who is the heart for which we seek.

3   Who is the holy mirror which shows us our responsibility.

4   Whose freedom grows in us when we surrender to him.

5   With whom I have to be united to resist the powers of the world.

[Guardini, Romano: Theologische Gebete
Josef Knecht, Frankfurt a.M., 1944, pp. 18–19]

PROVIDENCE

1   Whose wisdom rules over his whole creation.

2   From whom man got away and was lost.

3   Who overcame fate and called forth a new creation.

4   Who showed us God's face.

5   Who calls us to work in his kingdom as the one necessary thing.

[Guardini, Romano: Theologische Gebete
Josef Knecht, Frankfurt a.M., 1944, pp. 43–44]

CHRIST OUR KING!

1   To whom all kings will do homage.

2   Whom all nations will call blessed.

3   Who will save the lives of the needy.

4   Whose glorious name is blessed forever.

5   Whose glory will fill the whole world!

[Ps.72]

CONFIDENCE IN GOD'S PROTECTION

1   To whom on the mountain I lift my eyes.

2   Who does not permit your foot to slip.

3   Who does not slumber or sleep.

4   Who is your guardian and your shade.

5   Who will protect you from all harm.

[Ps. 121]

MY MISSION IN LIFE

1   Who created me for a definite service.

2   Who gave me a mission to perform.

3   Who made me a link in the chain of generations.

4   In whose wisdom I put all my trust.

5   Who knows what he is doing.

[Adapted from Cardinal Newman]

PAUL'S RELATIONSHIP TO CHRIST

1   Whose vision before Damascus taught Paul that the Messiah had come.

2   Who made Paul the apostle to the gentiles.

3   About whom Paul said: "The love of Christ urges me."

[2 Cor. 5:14]

4   In whose Cross alone Paul did boast.

[Gal. 6:14]

5   Who gave Paul the grace of martyrdom.

ISAIAH'S SONG OF THANKSGIVING

1 Who is the God of my salvation.

2 Who is my strength and my song.

3 At whose springs of salvation I shall draw water joyfully.

4 Whose deeds shall be made known among the nations.

5 Who is the Holy One of Israel.

[Is. 12:1–6]

CHARITY TOWARD OUR NEIGHBOR

1 Who said that charity covers all sins.

[Prv. 10:12]

2 Who wants us to cover the defects of others.

3 Who does not want us to speak against a brother.

4 Who wants me to pray for an erring brother.

5 Who will help me to deal lovingly with my neighbor.

LONGING FOR GOD

1   For whom my soul is thirsting.

2   Who fills my heart with longing.

3   Who appeases the hunger of my soul.

4   Who protects me in the shadow of his wings.

5   In whom alone my soul finds rest.

[Ps. 63]

HE RESCUES ALL WHO CLING TO HIM

1   Who is the refuge and fortress of those who abide in his
    shadow.

2   Who has delivered me from the snares of the fowlers.

3   Who is the stronghold in whom I trust.

4   Who has given command to his angels to guard me in all my
    ways.

5   Who rescues all those who cling to him and protects whoever
    knows his name.

[Ps. 91]

SAFETY IN GOD

1 Who is my light and my salvation.

2 Who is the fortress of my life.

3 Who will hide me deep in his tent.

4 Who fills my heart with courage.

5 Whose face my heart does seek.

[Ps. 27]

THE CALL OF CHRIST

1 Who calls us to anchor our faith in him.

2 Who calls us to enliven our images of hope in him.

3 Who calls us to love him with his heart.

4 Who calls us to become other Christs.

5 Who calls us to establish the Kingdom of God.

ON ENCOURAGEMENT DURING ADVERSITY

I

1 Who is the pilot in the deepest darkness.

2 Who is the reason never to abandon hope.

3 Who calms the raging waters by his rod.

4 Who often helps at the time of the worst extremities.

5 Who trains the patience of those who suffer.

II

1 Who permitted the three children to be cast into the fire.

2 Who displayed his power when all hope seemed gone.

3 Who converted the furnace to a temple of prayer.

4 Whom the three youth praised in a solemn song.

5 Whose resources and love are superabundant.

[St. John Chrysostom]

THE DIVINE PHYSICIAN

1 Who is the Divine Physician who cures our wounds.

2 Who is the fountain that lessens a fever.

3 Who is the justice that lifts our sin.

4 Who is the strength if you need help.

5 Who is the way if you long for heaven.

[St. Ambrose]

WISDOM OF THE HEART

1 Who often is next to you when you think he is far away.

[Thomas à Kempis]

2 Through whose strength I can do all things.

[St. Paul]

3 Who is always ready while we are not.

[Eckhart]

4 Who burdens nobody beyond his strength.

[Persian prv.]

5 In whom I withdraw when God seems to withdraw from the world.

[Middle ages]

GOD, MY ONLY TRUST

1   In whom alone my soul finds rest.

2   From whom comes my salvation.

3   Who is my rock and my fortress.

4   Who is the source of my hope.

5   Who will repay each man as his works deserve.

[Ps. 62]

RULES FOR CHRISTIAN CONDUCT

1   In whom we should rejoice always.

2   To whom we should pray unceasingly.

3   To whom we owe thanks for all things.

4   Who said to test everything.

5   Who want us to hold fast what is good.

[1 Thess. 5:16–22]

GOD AND MAN

1 Who is the infinite God . . . infinitely mysterious.

2 Who constitutes me in mysterious fashion.

3 Whose love is the basic foundation for our existence.

4 To whom we are on the way.

5 Who is the Trinitarian God.

[Karl Rahner, *Spiritual Exercises*, Ch. 1]

JESUS' HIDDEN LIFE

1 Whose hidden life was part of his messianic mission.

2 Whose life was hidden in God for thirty years.

3 Who practiced patience and waited for the Father.

4 Who transcended himself and was focused on the Father.

5 Who for thirty years lived what appeared outwardly as a useless life.

[Karl Rahner, *Spiritual Exercises*, Ch. 17]

THE CROSS

1   Who was a lover and remains a lover for all eternity.

2   Who came into the world to destroy death by his own death.

3   Who entered into our loneliness and embraces us with the outstretched arms of the Crucified.

4   Whose heart is open so that there might be a refuge for all sinners.

5   Whose heart was pierced so that streams of living water flow from it.

[Karl Rahner, *Spiritual Exercises*, Ch. 27]

TRANSFORMATION INTO CHRIST

1   Who wants to reproduce an incarnation of the Word in man.

2   Whose Holy Spirit can renew Christ's mystery in us.

3   Whose Holy Spirit gives us Christ's sanctity through grace.

4   Whose Holy Spirit takes us by the hand if we renew our efforts.

5   Whose sanctity consisted in conformity to the Father's will.

[Elizabeth of the Trinity]

GIVE US THIS DAY OUR DAILY BREAD

1   Who stands at the door and knocks.

2   Who wants to come in and sup with us.

3   Who deifies us by feeding us with the word of God.

4   Who strengthens our heart with the bread of life.

5   Who feeds us with bread from the tree of life.

[Origen]

FLIGHT FROM THE WORLD

1   Who teaches flight from the world and pursuit of God.

2   Whose true follower clings to God alone.

3   Who imprints the image of God on the man who flees from sin.

4   Who offers us the ladder of virtues to get to heaven.

5   Who calls us to forsake the smoke and to strive after the light.

[St. Ambrose]

EPILOGUE: THE NEW HEAVEN AND THE NEW EARTH

I

1 Who will create a new heaven and a new earth.

2 Who will make his dwelling among us.

3 Who "makes all things new"!

4 Who shall wipe every tear from their eyes.

5 Who will give those who thirst water from the spring of life-giving water.

[Rev. 21:1–6]

II

1 Who will give his gifts to the victor.

2 Who showed John the new Jerusalem.

3 Who is the Lamp and the Light of the new creation.

4 By whose Light all nations shall walk.

5 From whose throne flowed the river of life-giving water.

[Rev. 21:7–22:1]

TO FACILITATE THIS WAY OF MEDITATING,
YOU MAY CUT OUT THIS SHEET AND LAMINATE IT
TO MAKE IT MORE DURABLE

STRUCTURE OF PRAYER USED IN THIS BOOK:

ONE OUR FATHER,
TEN TIMES THE MEDITATION FRAME,
IN THE CENTER OF WHICH
INSERT MEDITATION PROPER.
GLORY BE TO THE FATHER ETC . . .

REPEAT THE ABOVE FOR EACH OF THE
FIVE MEDITATIONS GIVEN IN
EACH SET OF MEDITATIONS.

THE MEDITATION FRAMES
READ:

Regular one: PRAISED BE THE LORD, THE
                         HOLY AND MIGHTY,
                      THE SON OF THE LIVING GOD,
                         WHO . . .
                      insert meditation proper . . .
                      JESUS CHRIST, SAVIOUR OF
                         THE WORLD,
                      OUR MASTER AND OUR
                         BROTHER,
                      HAVE MERCY ON US.

                             ∿

LONGER Petition: JESUS CHRIST, SAVIOUR OF THE
                         WORLD,
                      LEAD US THE GOOD WAY,
                      AND AFTER OUR DEATH
                      BE A MERCIFUL JUDGE TO US.

                             ∿

GOOD FRIDAY   HOLY IS GOD!
PETITION: HOLY AND STRONG!
                      HOLY IMMORTAL ONE!
                      HAVE MERCY ON US!